Write to Know Series

Secondary

Nonfiction Writing Prompts for

Biology

T5-CCX-993

- Carl G. Gatton, B.S.
- Rosemary Ruthven, M.S., Literacy Specialist
- Edited by Amy M. Whited, M.A.

A L P
Advanced
Learning
Press

A L P
Advanced
Learning
   Press

Advanced Learning Press
317 Inverness Way South, Suite 150
Englewood, CO 80112
Phone (800) 844-6599 or (303) 504-9312 ■ Fax (303) 504-9417
www.AdvancedLearningPress.com

Copyright © 2005
Advanced Learning Centers, Inc.

All rights reserved. No part of this publication may be reproduced, stored in a retrieval system, or transmitted in any form or by any means, electronic, mechanical, photocopying, recording, scanning, or otherwise, except as permitted by law, without the prior written permission of the Publisher.

Limited Reproduction Permission: Permission is hereby granted for individual teachers and educators to reproduce the prompts for classroom use. Reproduction of these materials for an entire school system is strictly forbidden.

Notice of Liability: The information in this book is distributed on an "As Is" basis, without warranty. While every precaution has been taken in the preparation of the book, neither the authors nor Advanced Learning Centers, Inc., shall have any liability to any person or entity with respect to any loss or damage caused or alleged to be caused directly or indirectly by the instructions contained in this book.

Advanced Learning Press also publishes books in a variety of electronic formats. Some content that appears in print may not be available in electronic books.

ISBN: 1-933196-17-3

Printed in the United States of America

10 09 08 07 06 05   01 02 03 04 05 06 07 08 09

CONTENTS

Why nonfiction prompts?

Giving students reasons to write across the curriculum is one of the most powerful and time-saving strategies in the educator's toolkit. The content areas present numerous opportunities for students to engage in writing for authentic purposes; in turn, writing is an excellent vehicle for students to demonstrate their understandings of the essential concepts being taught in a content area. These prompts have been written for teachers who are committed to standards-based instruction and to integrating their curriculum. They were selected to complement (History/Social Studies/Science/Math) units of study and to give students practice in all four domains of writing.

How do I use them?

Teachers may choose to use the prompts in a variety of ways:

- As *writing-process* assignments, wherein students have several weeks to synthesize and apply essential understandings of new concepts to a quality piece of writing.

- For teacher-guided *interactive writing* lessons, during which teachers can reinforce content-area learning while also assisting students to refine their writing techniques.

- As *performance assessments,* wherein students demonstrate they can effectively answer essential questions generated from a unit of study in a content area.

- In some cases, as a *quick-write pretest* to assess students' preexisting knowledge before commencement of a unit.

When not to use them

Although some prompts could be given as quick-write assessments of students' preexisting knowledge, these prompts should be given primarily during or upon completion of a unit of study. They are not designed to be given "cold" as a test instrument to assess student writing proficiency. Clearly, if these prompts are given prior to instruction, students' writing scores will potentially be undermined by their inability to support their ideas with relevant facts and details.

Why is the wording so sophisticated?

You will note that the wording used in the prompts often mirrors that found in the standards themselves. Such terminology will be intimidating to students only if there are no strong learning associations with the meaning of the words. Kindergartners have no problems remembering what a *Tyrannosaurus rex* is; with sound instruction, nor do they have difficulty understanding terms such as *evaporation*.

Some prompts don't exactly fit the content I taught

These prompts are suggestions and a place to start. Teachers are encouraged to modify the wording of these prompts, or write their own prompts, to better fit the emphasis of the unit and the purpose of the writing. For example, they may wish to vary the number of paragraphs required, depending on what part of the year the unit was completed. They may feel that students would do better responding to the prompt in the form of a poem or a letter rather than a straight composition. Keep two important things in mind, however: students need practice in all four domains of writing, and the content taught must be standards-based.

What should I consider when writing my own prompts or when modifying existing prompts?

The wording of a prompt can either motivate or intimidate a writer. Good prompts make it very clear to students what you are asking of them. Compare the following two prompts:

1. *Explain precipitation and evaporation in at least two paragraphs.*

2. *Your friend doesn't know how there is always enough water stored in the sky to fall as rain. She also doesn't know how puddles on the playground can just disappear after a while. Write a report of at least two paragraphs to help your friend understand precipitation and evaporation.*

Prompts like the first one tend to reinforce a student's notion that writing is what one does to pass a test or complete an assignment for a grade. By contrast, the second prompt takes the following points into consideration:

- The audience for whom the student is writing is clear (a friend).

- The purpose of the writing has been specified (to help the friend understand).

- The type of writing required is referred to as a "report," reminding students that this piece of writing should be presented as straightforward prose and will not be, for example, in a letter, poem, or story format.

- The minimum number of paragraphs/sentences required has been specified.

- Some clues have been put into the prompt by way of the scenario to assist students in activating their existing knowledge on the subject.

Some other things to consider when writing prompts:

- If you are creating the prompt specifically to assess student knowledge about a content area at the end of a unit of study, design the prompt around the essential question(s) you began with at the start of the unit.

- Don't ask students to talk about anything personal that may be seen as an invasion of privacy.

- Avoid asking students to write specifically about holidays (e.g., Halloween, Christmas) or birthdays. These can be sensitive areas for some students and their parents because of religious beliefs or negative feelings about holidays.

- Be sure you could effectively write to the prompt yourself. Plan out what you would do, as an expert writer, to satisfy the requirements of the prompt.

- Write prompts that will give students practice in all four domains of writing.

What are the four domains of writing students need to practice, and why is it important for teachers to know what they are?

We use the *sensory/descriptive* domain when we write down our deepest feelings in a diary or use our five senses to describe an unusual sea creature for a scientific journal. We enjoy *imaginative/narrative* writing every time we read a novel, watch a television drama, or catch a movie. When we fill out forms, make to-do lists, summarize documents, or write directions, we are using the *practical/informative* domain. We dive into the *analytical/expository* domain when we write a campaign speech, justify an opinion, or e-mail friends convincing them to go to the holiday destination of our choosing.

The majority of writing we do in life falls under the *practical/informative* and *analytical/expository* domains—but at times those domains will contain elements of the other two. For example, a report on the results of an experiment will be more effective if it contains good sensory description; a historical novel can be a source of practical information while also being an imaginative narrative. Hence, it is vital for students to receive instruction and practice in *all four* domains. Moreover, it is crucial for students and teachers to know that although a piece may contain several elements spanning more than one domain, ultimately it is categorized by its *primary* objective. The following table gives definitions and examples of each domain.

The Domain	Its Primary Objective	Some Examples
Sensory/Descriptive	To describe an object, a moment in time, or feelings experienced in vivid, sensory detail.	• Detailed recordings of observations made of a fossil • A poem describing feelings experienced after suffering an injustice • A character sketch of Abraham Lincoln
Imaginative/Narrative	To tell what happened in a logical sequence. This could be a real-life or imaginary series of events.	• The autobiography of Thomas Edison • The story of Charlie Crawley, who started out as a caterpillar and ended up as a butterfly • A comic strip portraying Newton's discovery of gravity
Practical/Informative	To present basic information with clarity.	• A business letter to the supplier of the canteen milk cartons informing them of leaks • Step-by step instructions for performing an experiment • A summary of a *National Geographic* article
Analytical/Expository	To explain, analyze, compare and contrast, or persuade.	• A television commercial persuading viewers to recycle their soda cans • An explanation of the impact of the Gold Rush on life choices made by Chinese immigrants • A comparison of sedimentary and igneous rocks

What kind of scoring guide should I use to evaluate proficiency?

Whatever scoring guide or rubric you decide to use, ensure that the *students* know the criteria being used to assess proficiency. Those criteria may be embodied in an existing scoring guide or one you and the students have created together around the demands of a specific prompt.

Decide what you are *primarily* evaluating. Are you mainly trying to determine whether students have internalized information and acquired essential understandings, or are you evaluating *how well* they are able to use language to express what they know? Ultimately, of course, your objective is to develop proficiency in both. Certainly, if a prompt were given as a writing-process assignment to be completed over several weeks, you should reasonably expect *both* excellent content and excellent written expression to be evident. If, however, the prompt is given as a posttest at the conclusion of a unit, you may choose not to heavily penalize mistakes in sentence structure and conventions, as long as students demonstrate essential understanding(s) of the content. If you are more concerned with a student's ability to state and justify an opinion in a quick-write assignment, you may choose on that occasion not to heavily penalize inaccurate information.

The following are samples of an analytic scoring guide and a holistic scoring guide. An *analytic scoring* guide allows you to assess a student's writing proficiency trait by trait. Simply give a 1, 2, 3, or 4 score for each trait; a "3" score indicates proficiency in that area. An analytic scoring guide enables teachers to focus their instruction on those areas of writing in which a student is not yet proficient. In other words, the assessment informs instruction. The *holistic scoring guide,* in contrast, is less specific and gives the student a score based on the teacher's overall impression of the piece. As with the analytic scoring guide, a "3" is considered a proficient score.

Middle and Secondary Analytic Scoring Guide

TRAIT	4 Exceeds Grade-Level Expectations	3 Proficient	2 Approaching Proficiency	1 Not Proficient
Essential understandings of content	Clearly demonstrates essential understanding(s). Provides strong, credible support of the topic and shares insights that go beyond the obvious and predictable. Maintains a consistent point of view.	Demonstrates essential understanding(s). Supporting details and ideas may at times be too general or out of balance with the main idea. Maintains a mostly consistent point of view.	An attempt was made to address the main idea, but the essential understanding(s) are not clear. Attempts are made to support ideas, but may be irrelevant. Inconsistent point of view.	Ideas are unclear and lack a central link to essential understanding(s).

Middle and Secondary Analytic Scoring Guide *(Continued)*

TRAIT	4 Exceeds Grade-Level Expectations	3 Proficient	2 Approaching Proficiency	1 Not Proficient
Organization	Uses an organizational structure that fits the purpose of the writing task. Constructs inviting introductions and satisfying conclusions. Selects effective transitions and employs purposeful pacing.	Uses an organizational structure that fits the purpose of the writing task. Creates clear introductions and conclusions. Transitions are adequate, but pacing may be inconsistent.	Uses an organizational structure that addresses only parts of the writing task. Has undeveloped beginnings and/or conclusions and weak or overused transitions. Little knowledge of pacing.	Uses an organizational structure that may be haphazard and disjointed. Has weak beginning and conclusion.

Middle and Secondary Analytic Scoring Guide *(Continued)*

TRAIT	4 Exceeds Grade-Level Expectations	3 Proficient	2 Approaching Proficiency	1 Not Proficient
Content Vocabulary	Demonstrates understanding of vocabulary related to content. Uses words in an interesting, precise, and natural way. Uses fresh and lively expressions that at times include figurative language or slang.	Demonstrates understanding of vocabulary related to content. Uses words in a precise and natural way appropriate to audience and purpose.	Attempts to use content vocabulary words, but does not apply them appropriately. Words used are generally imprecise and at times may not be appropriate to audience and purpose.	Words are limited, monotonous, or misused. Only the most general kind of message is communicated.

TRAIT	4 **Exceeds Grade-Level Expectations**	3 **Proficient**	2 **Approaching Proficiency**	1 **Not Proficient**
Voice	Demonstrates strong audience awareness and creates a strong interaction with the reader. There is a strong sense of commitment to the topic. An appropriate voice or tone is consistently employed. Topic is brought to life through conviction, excitement, or humor.	Demonstrates audience awareness; there is a sense of commitment to the topic most of the time.	Demonstrates limited audience awareness; the sense of commitment to the topic is inconsistent. Uses a voice that is overly informal or impersonal and flat.	Shows no audience awareness. It is hard to sense the person and purpose behind the words. Voice is consistently flat.

TRAIT	4 Exceeds Grade-Level Expectations	3 Proficient	2 Approaching Proficiency	1 Not Proficient
Sentence fluency	Sentences are well constructed with correct word order and subject/verb agreement; there are no run-ons or fragments. Employs correct tenses and uses pronouns correctly. Varies sentence structure, length, and beginnings to strengthen the meaning of the text and draw attention to the main ideas.	Uses complete sentences. Occasional errors in word order, tense, pronoun usage, subject/verb agreement, or use of run-ons and fragments do not detract from meaning. Varies sentence length and beginnings.	Errors in word order, pronoun usage, tense, subject/verb agreement, and/or use of run-ons and fragments detract from meaning. The sentence structure tends to be mechanical rather than fluid.	Errors in sentence structure obscure meaning and often cause the reader to slow down or reread.

TRAIT	4 **Exceeds Grade-Level Expectations**	3 **Proficient**	2 **Approaching Proficiency**	1 **Not Proficient**
Conventions	Strong control of standard writing conventions. Little editing is needed. Uses correct grammar and usage to enhance communication and contribute to clarity and style. Consistently uses paragraph breaks that reinforce organization and meaning.	Reasonable control of standard writing conventions. Occasional errors in capitalization, punctuation, and spelling do not interfere with readability. Grammar and usage guide the reader through the text. Employs paragraph breaks that reinforce organization and meaning.	Makes frequent capitalization, punctuation, and/or spelling errors that distract the reader. Errors in grammar and usage interfere with readability and meaning. Paragraph breaks may not effectively contribute to organization and meaning.	Shows little control of standard writing conventions. Errors in grammar and usage block the meaning of the writing, making it difficult to focus on the message.

Student Name: _____ Date: _____

Middle and Secondary Holistic Scoring Guide

4—Exceeds Grade-Level Expectations

- Demonstrates essential understanding(s) about the content and gives supporting details that go beyond the predictable. Maintains a consistent point of view.

- Uses an organizational structure that fits the purpose of the writing task. Constructs inviting introductions and satisfying conclusions. Consistently uses paragraph breaks that reinforce organization and meaning. Uses effective transitions and pacing that move the reader easily through the text.

- Demonstrates understanding of vocabulary related to content. Uses fresh and lively expressions that at times include figurative language or slang.

- Demonstrates strong audience awareness; there is a sense of a person and a purpose behind the words. Consistently employs an appropriate voice or tone. Brings topic to life through conviction, excitement, or humor; there is a strong interaction with the reader.

- Demonstrates stylistic control. The sentence structure strengthens the meaning of the text and draws attention to key ideas. Correct grammar and usage contribute to clarity and style. Little editing is needed.

3—Proficient

- Demonstrates essential understanding(s) about the content. Supporting details and ideas may at times be too general or out of balance with the main idea, but maintains a consistent point of view.

- Uses an organizational structure that fits the purpose of the writing task. Creates clear introductions and conclusions. Employs paragraph breaks that generally reinforce organization and meaning. Uses adequate transitions. Pacing may be inconsistent.

- Demonstrates understanding of vocabulary related to content. Uses words in an interesting, precise, and natural way appropriate to audience and purpose.

- Demonstrates audience awareness; there is a sense of a person and purpose behind the words. Employs an appropriate voice or tone most of the time.

- Demonstrates reasonable control of standard writing conventions. Some syntax, spelling, capitalization, and punctuation errors occur, but do not interfere with meaning.

2—Approaching Proficiency

- Attempts to address the main idea, but does *not* demonstrate essential understanding(s) about the content.

- Made an attempt to organize the text, but the overall structure may be inconsistent or not appropriate for the writing task. May use an introduction or conclusion. Sequence of ideas may not be effectively presented.

- Attempts to use content vocabulary words, but does not apply them appropriately. Words used are generally imprecise and at times may not be appropriate to audience and purpose.

- Demonstrates limited audience awareness; there is little sense of a person and purpose behind the words. Uses a voice that is overly informal or impersonal and flat. There is little sense of "writing to be read."

- Demonstrates limited control of standard conventions. The sentence structure may be mechanical rather than fluid. Frequent errors in syntax, spelling, capitalization, and punctuation detract from meaning.

1—Not Proficient

- Ideas are unclear and lack a central link to essential understanding(s).

- Organizational structure is not appropriate for the purpose. Weak beginning and/or conclusion. No logical sequence of ideas.

- Words are limited, monotonous, and/or misused. Only the most general kind of message is communicated.

- Shows no audience awareness; it is hard to sense a person and purpose behind the words.

- Little control of standard conventions. Errors in syntax, spelling, capitalization, and punctuation obscure meaning, making it difficult for the reader to focus on the message.

How can I help students evaluate and improve their own writing performance?

Receiving specific feedback from teachers, especially during a one-to-one conference, is critical for improving student writing. It is equally important to give students opportunities to confer with each other. Students soon find out how well they are communicating their knowledge in a piece of writing when fellow students tell them some portion of it doesn't make sense. Additionally, the process of evaluating the writing of others helps the students doing the evaluating to focus attention on their own strengths and weaknesses. The deliberate acts of thinking about, and evaluating, our own learning and learning processes is known as metacognition. Encouraging this kind of self-reflection in students is crucial if we want them to become independent learners and effective communicators. Peer conferencing allows students to explain what they learned and how they learned it, which not only helps to anchor new concepts in memory, but also provides the foundation and scaffolding on which to build further learning. This sharing of knowledge, ideas, and processes has the added benefit of contributing positively to overall class performance.

When asking a student to evaluate another student's writing, it is essential, first, to define the criteria by which the piece is to be judged, and second, to establish some conferencing guidelines. If this is not done, the feedback may be either too vague or too brutal to be constructive. The following "house rules" are worth modeling, discussing, and even posting for the class:

1. I will read the piece through, using stick-on notes or flags to mark those areas I want to discuss with the author afterward.

2. I will give careful thought to the written evaluation I complete so that my colleague will know in which areas proficiency has or has not been achieved.

3. I will not make any marks or corrections on the piece itself. Any changes I suggest will be made by the author's hand only, after the author has accepted them.

4. I will back up my praise or concerns about the writing with evidence from the piece.

5. I will help the author to understand how to communicate essential concepts more effectively.

Peer Evaluation and Conferencing Form

Title of Piece: _____ Written by: _____

Evaluator: _____ Date: _____

Facet of Writing	The piece is proficient in this area, as evidenced by...	The piece is not yet proficient in this area, as evidenced by...
Content Demonstrates understanding of the essential concepts needed to write to the prompt. Gives supporting details that help get the point across. Maintains a consistent point of view.		

Facet of Writing	The piece is proficient in this area, as evidenced by...	The piece is not yet proficient in this area, as evidenced by...
Organization Uses an organizational structure that fits the purpose of the writing task. Creates clear introductions and conclusions. Transitions are adequate and the pacing is consistent.		
Content Vocabulary Demonstrates understanding of vocabulary words related to the subject. Uses these and other words in a precise and natural way appropriate to the audience and purpose.		

Facet of Writing	The piece is proficient in this area, as evidenced by...	The piece is not yet proficient in this area, as evidenced by...
Voice Demonstrates audience awareness; there is a sense of commitment to the topic.		
Sentence Fluency Uses complete sentences and varies sentence structure, length, and beginnings.		

NONFICTION WRITING FOR BIOLOGY

Facet of Writing	The piece is proficient in this area, as evidenced by...	The piece is not yet proficient in this area, as evidenced by...
Conventions Grammar and usage guide the reader through the text. Employs paragraph breaks that reinforce organization and meaning. Spelling, capitalization, and punctuation are mostly correct.		

The middle ground, where both reason and research are found, is that while demographic factors such as poverty and second languages are clearly associated with lower student performance, the impact of these factors is less than the impact of great teaching and school leadership.

—Douglas B. Reeves, Ph.D. (2004, p. 170)

A few years ago, a meteorite was discovered in the Antarctic, and it was later determined to be material ejected from the planet Mars by an asteroid strike. Some scientists thought that the meteorite contained fossilized single-cell organisms. Write a school newspaper article that explains what is meant by a cell. Describe some of the major life functions that must take place in a living cell.

*Although they have important roles to play in adolescents'
literacy development, language arts and reading teachers
need content-area teachers to show students how to read
and write like a scientist, historian, or mathematician.*

—Richard Vacca (2002, p. 10)

Think about how you feed yourself. You take in solid and liquid nourishment for energy and growth. You are fairly selective in what you eat and drink. In reality, you are feeding the billions of cells that make up your body. Write a narrative about how living cells are nourished. What parts of the cell are responsible for selecting only certain molecules and rejecting others? What specialized chemicals are produced by the cell to break down food molecules into substances suitable for cellular nourishment?

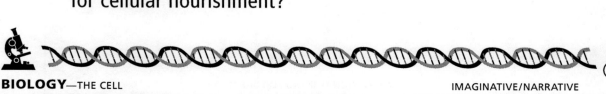

Content literacy is often defined as the level of reading and writing skill that learners need in an academic subject to comprehend and respond to ideas in text used for instructional purposes.

—Richard Vacca (2002, p. 7)

Even though a cell is the smallest unit of life, it conducts many complex internal biochemical processes, such as respiration, energy storage, energy utilization, and reproduction. These processes do not take place in random or chaotic fashion. Write a description of the internal "programming structure" that directs the functions of the cell.

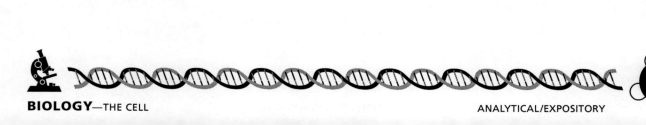

An effective accountability system must answer at least four common sense questions: one about individual student achievement; a second about school performance; a third about ways to help students learn; and a fourth about determining educational effectiveness.

—Douglas B. Reeves, Ph.D. (2004, p. 26)

NONFICTION WRITING FOR BIOLOGY

Some specialized cells contain structures that use solar energy to complete the chemical processes necessary to maintain the cells' life functions. Suppose another student asks you about this process. Explain to the student how this process works in nature. Be sure to include the proper scientific names for the process and for the cellular component that makes this process possible.

ANALYTICAL/EXPOSITORY

Clear, accessible instructional rubrics can give students repeated practice with planning, revising, and editing.

—Bruce Saddler and Heidi Andrade (2004, p. 51)

Cells are classified as *procaryotic* or *eucaryotic*. Define these two terms, and then sketch diagrams of the two types of cells. List the major differences between the cell types and label the major internal components of the cells. Which type of cell is found in animal life?

In response to the diverse needs of its students, a school district must be committed to maintaining equity and must set high standards and expectations for all students.

—Douglas B. Reeves, Ph.D. (2004, p. 94)

Describe the method of reproduction of bacteria. Draw a sequence diagram showing the progression of cellular division. How does this process differ from that of animal-cell reproduction?

ANALYTICAL/EXPOSITORY

Fairness and accountability are not about "beating" someone else, but they are certainly about winning the battle against inequity, injustice and ignorance.

—Douglas B. Reeves, Ph.D. (2004, p. 100)

The head of a pin is about 2 mm in diameter. A typical bacterial cell is about 1 micrometer in diameter. Your biology teacher has instructed you to collect the appropriate number of typical bacterial cells (no pathogens, please!) and place them side-by-side across the head of a pin. How many bacteria can you lay across a pin head in this manner? Explain how you arrived at your answer.

Accountability systems that fail to recognize the importance of teaching ... will fail to achieve their primary objective: the improvement of student learning.

—Douglas B. Reeves, Ph.D. (2004, p. 58)

DNA and RNA molecules are large chains of structural units called *nucleotides.* Explain the term *nucleotide.* Draw a diagram of the chemical structure that forms a nucleotide. Label each of the three compounds in the nucleotide.

For learning, the act of writing provides a chronology of our thoughts, which we can then label, objectify, modify, or build on[,] and it engages us in becoming invested in our ideas and learning. Writing-to-learn forms and extends thinking and thus deepens understanding.... Like reading-to-learn, it is a meaning-making process.

—Vicki Jacobs (2002, p. 60)

A *nucleobase* is an organic compound that makes up one of the three chemical structures required for the creation of a nucleotide. Create a table that lists the five nucleobases by name, along with each base's single-letter representation.

ANALYTICAL/EXPOSITORY

The principles and practices of secondary reading and writing provide means by which students can move from understanding to demonstrating understanding.

—Vicki Jacobs (2002, p. 61)

Nucleobases bond together in specific combinations to form *base pairs.* Make a table that illustrates which nucleobases form pairs. There is one nucleobase out of five that is not found in the DNA molecule. Which one is it?

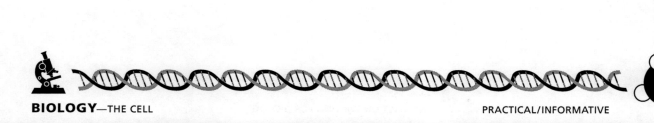

Writing for social action is an ideal way to energize students, especially students who see school as pointless and dull.

—Randy Boomer (2004, p. 34)

In your own words, explain the three components of the *cell theory*, which is a basic concept of biology.

*Writing should involve discovering, analyzing, synthesizing
and evaluating—not just copying and downloading.*

—Michael M. Yell (2002, p. 66)

50

Some single-celled microorganisms form spores to protect themselves from adverse environmental conditions. Describe some of the environmental factors that you think would cause the formation of spores in a population of bacteria.

SENSORY/DESCRIPTIVE

Learning to write means learning to speak out, to make one's voice heard in the great human conversation. And by teaching students to raise their voices through writing on social issues that concern them, we teach them to participate actively in a democracy.

—Randy Boomer (2004, p. 34)

What is the main function of the Golgi apparatus in a eucaryotic cell? Explain your answer.

ANALYTICAL/EXPOSITORY

Great teachers know only too well that writing is hard work—exhausting for students and massively time consuming for teachers. But they also understand that if students are to make knowledge their own, they must wrestle with facts, struggle with details, and rework raw information into language that reaches an audience.

—Laurel Schmidt (2004, p. 45)

Humans and other animals are classified as multicellular organisms. Explain the term *multicellular.* Discuss some of the functions performed by the cells of your body.

The persons responsible for the education of our children must have a clear idea of what they must do to help all students achieve.

—Douglas B. Reeves, Ph.D. (2004, p. 96)

A multicellular organism, such as a dog or a kitten, is made up of many specialized cells that form tissues and organs in distinct ways. Something within the cell has the information for determining the animal's characteristics, such as eye color and fur or hair color patterns. Describe the components of the DNA molecule that have the unique program for producing individual characteristics in multicellular organisms.

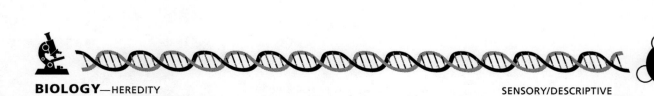

BIOLOGY—HEREDITY

SENSORY/DESCRIPTIVE

*Only with a written response from students can teachers
create the strategies necessary to improve performance for
both teachers and learner.*

—Douglas B. Reeves, Ph.D. (2004, p. 190)

Draw a diagram of the following nucleotide sequence:

ATGCCGAT

Your mission is to create a complementary sequence. Draw your resulting sequence and explain why the nucleotides almost always combine in predictable ways. Explain which nucleotides always join together. Write the names of the four nucleotides. Explain some things that might cause the wrong sequence to be formed.

*Helping writers develop fluency and competence in
a variety of technologies is a key part of teaching writing
in this century.*

—Kathleen Blake Yancey (2004, p. 38)

Chromosomes are unique structures located on the DNA molecule. Every living thing has a fixed number of chromosomes. For example, we humans have 44, chimpanzees have 48, and a carrot has 18. Explain why chromosomes are present in the DNA molecule in even numbers.

ANALYTICAL/EXPOSITORY

For subject teachers to implement principles and practices of secondary reading and writing[,] they must first recognize reading and writing as meaning-making processes that can support their instructional goals, particularly those related to understanding content.

—Vicki Jacobs (2002, p. 61)

62

Sexual reproduction takes place in both the animal and plant kingdoms. Explain how the fertilized egg receives its genetic information. What is the scientific name of the fertilized egg? Are the offspring exact duplicates of the parent cells? Why or why not? Explain your answer.

PRACTICAL/INFORMATIVE

Effective assessment is the foundation of effective accountability.

—Douglas B. Reeves, Ph.D. (2004, p. 17)

Some life forms reproduce asexually. Describe the difference between *sexual* and *asexual* reproduction. Include some examples of plants and microorganisms that reproduce by asexual reproduction.

In order to provide useful information about student achievement, an accountability system must be based on clear standards that have been communicated to students, parents, teachers, and other district stakeholders.

—Douglas B. Reeves, Ph.D. (2004, p. 26)

There are two copies of 22 chromosomes in a human cell, resulting in 44 chromosomes total. A pair of chromosomes contains the coding to determine the sex of the offspring. Explain the significance of X chromosomes and Y chromosomes.

Teachers can develop reflective critics within their classrooms by teaching students how to use rubrics to assess their own and their classmates' writing. Student assessment has the additional advantage of promoting self regulation because it gives students some of the responsibility for judging written work instead of placing that responsibility solely on the teacher.

—Bruce Saddler and Heidi Andrade (2004, p. 51)

68

Modern genetic understanding can be traced to the early work of Gregor Mendel. Write a press release outlining Mendel's findings and contributions concerning pea-plant genetics.

As a matter of fairness and good educational practice, students deserve to have their work evaluated against an objective standard.

—Douglas B. Reeves, Ph.D. (2004, p. 34)

What is a Punnett square? How is it used in genetic research? Draw a Punnett square and explain its use.

When teachers embed writing strategies in instruction, they enrich and enliven the required curriculum.

—Michael M. Yell (2002, p. 66)

Explain the difference between a *genotype* and a *phenotype.* Give an example of how each is expressed in a living being.

When we give students freedom to take risks, a stake in their own progress and the language to understand the writing process, their fear of writing will turn to true excitement.

—Natalia Perchemlides and Carolyn Coutant (2004, p. 56)

Explain how one of your unique characteristics, such as eye color, is a result of very specific biochemical instructions. What is the source of these instructions?

75

The more we write and talk, the more we have to write and say.

—Peter Elbow (2004, p. 13)

NONFICTION WRITING FOR BIOLOGY

What do you think might occur if an error is made in the base arrangement while DNA transcription is occurring? Explain.

Students who write with confidence will be more open to strategies that allow them to express their written voice.

—Tom Romano (2004, p. 20)

If DNA contains the hereditary information within its nucleotide polymer, what is the information used for within the RNA structure? Explain your answer.

ANALYTICAL/EXPOSITORY

Effective accountability systems . . . are "done-for" teachers and students: to enhance their interaction and improve student learning.

—Douglas B. Reeves, Ph.D. (2004, p. 49)

Earth's natural processes tend to take place in a series of repeating cyclical loops, such as the hydrologic cycle. Draw a concept diagram that shows how living things are part of a recycling loop. Write a scenario about what happens to dead organic material as it is broken down into simpler substances. Think about other life forms that aid in this process. Explain what the surface of our planet would be like without decomposers!

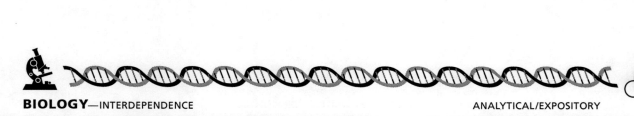

*Achievement comes from a focus on clear standards,
not from the inappropriate complacency that results from
short-term victories over classmates.*

—Douglas B. Reeves, Ph.D. (2004, p. 37)

The ultimate source of energy to support life on our planet comes from our local star, the sun. Without sunlight, plant life could not exist in its present form. Draw a diagram showing the energy flow from the sun and how this energy is used by ecosystems. Explain the interdependence of life within the ecosystem.

The word "strategy" often connotes lofty vision and grand plans; in fact, it is simply a method of achieving a result.

—Douglas B. Reeves, Ph.D. (2004, p. 16)

84

Write a narrative on what you have read or heard recently about the human impact on Earth's ecosystems. What do you think we can do to ensure that the natural systems will survive and be sustainable for the future?

BIOLOGY—INTERDEPENDENCE

IMAGINATIVE/NARRATIVE

When students are knee-deep in the process of composing, they need feedback from both teachers and peers.

—Natalia Perchemlides and Carolyn Coutant (2004, p. 54)

Many life forms rely on either living or dead organisms for nutrients and energy. Make a table with two headings, one for *parasites* and the other for *saprophytes.* Define the two headings and make a list of at least five examples of each. Try to think of things from your daily life that fit your definitions.

Without the writer's mindful involvement, the writing process is like a ship without a rudder—in motion, but out of control.

—Bruce Saddler and Heidi Andrade (2004, p. 48)

You have probably heard or read in the news about the concern over extinction of species by habitat loss, pollution, and other anthropological and natural factors. Describe how the loss of a species can have an undesirable effect on the surviving organisms in a food web.

All teachers in all subjects share the responsibility for literacy development in middle and high school.

—Richard Vacca (2002, p. 10)

Groups of organisms often live in a close-knit environment. Explain the term *symbiotic partnership* within the context of an ecosystem. Include some examples of this arrangement found in nature.

Students need frequent feedback about their performances as compared with clear, objective standards—not as compared with the performance of their peers.

—Douglas B. Reeves, Ph.D. (2004, p. 38)

NONFICTION WRITING FOR BIOLOGY

Describe a food chain. Think about how energy is transferred from one organism to another within the chain. Place the organisms presented here into the correct sequence for a food chain: squirrel, fox, walnut, cougar.

DESCRIPTIVE/SENSORY

The purpose of accountability is to improve student achievement.

—Douglas B. Reeves, Ph.D. (2004, p. 41)

Explain the difference between a *food chain* and a *food web*. What is the ultimate source of energy that powers food chains and food webs?

ANALYTICAL/EXPOSITORY

Peer assessment helps students reflect on their own writing, recognize dissonances, and create solutions.

—Natalie Perchemlides and Carolyn Coutant (2004, p. 55)

Imagine that the sunlight reaching the Earth's surface was significantly reduced for a three-month period. Write a short story about how this would affect your life and the plant and animal life on this planet. Be sure to use your scientific knowledge of biology and life science as a basis for the story.

The central focus of a standards-based system is the achievement of standards by as many students as possible.

—Douglas B. Reeves, Ph.D. (2004, p. 180)

Describe the process of *photosynthesis.* What is the source of energy for photosynthesis? What roles do carbon, hydrogen, and oxygen have in the process? Write the chemical equation involving carbon dioxide and water and the resulting organic compound and gas produced by photosynthesis.

ANALYTICAL/EXPOSITORY

[A]ccountability information can offer teachers and school leaders insights into effective practices to improve student achievement.

—Douglas B. Reeves, Ph.D. (2004, p. 170)

Energy for cellular respiration is stored in molecules of an organic compound with the acronym ATP. Write an explanation of the term *ATP*. Describe what happens to the ATP molecule when it donates energy to a cell. What is the name of the new compound that is formed by this breakdown process?

Good writing, regardless of the mode of discourse, causes writers to think. That thinking involves a productive dialectic between analysis and synthesis.

—Tom Romano (1995, p. 6)

Multicellular organisms respond to temperature, light, moisture, presence or absence of nutrients, and danger from other predatory organisms. Write an explanation of how you think that multicellular organisms developed the capabilities to cope with changes in their immediate environment. Hint: Think about hereditary and learned responses.

ANALYTICAL/EXPOSITORY

Teacher assessment gives a more comprehensive view of student performance than a single test score.

—Douglas B. Reeves, Ph.D. (2004, p. 55)

A fellow student has asked, "Where is the supporting evidence that life has evolved over millions of years?" Write a response to this question. Where on Earth would you find ancient records that support this concept?

Student writers need a standard to work toward. In a class in which students evaluate themselves, evaluative modules provide a standard of quality.

—Natalia Perchemlides and Carolyn Coutant (2004, p. 55)

Imagine that you have arrived on another planet and have been assigned the task of systematically classifying the living creatures found there. Write a description of one of these imaginary creatures. Design a hypothetical classification key all the way down to the species level.

ANALYTICAL/EXPOSITORY

Good teachers realize that a major part of teaching is helping kids understand themselves as learners and helping them begin to think like professionals in whatever discipline they are studying.

—Marcia D'Arcangelo (2002, p. 12)

Imagine that you are a time traveler. You have chosen to visit a period that is 10,000 years in the future. Based on what you understand at this point in your education about biological evolution, write a scenario about how humans might evolve. Take into consideration the present events on Earth, such as natural resources and environmental trends.

The effective use of accountability data requires the commonplace use of research, assessment, and communication by teachers and school leaders.

—Douglas B. Reeves, Ph.D. (2004, p. 175)

Create a concept map for the naturalist Charles Darwin. How did his theory contribute to the understanding of biological evolution? Where did he get his idea?

Students should never have to wander aimlessly through their educational journeys, wondering what they need to do in order to please the teacher.

—Douglas B. Reeves, Ph.D. (2004, p. 33)

Over a long period of millions of years, animal and plant life forms can show changes in morphology. Explain what causes these changes.

Writing helps students think about the content, reflect on their knowledge of the content, and share their thoughts with the teacher.

—Douglas Fisher, Nancy Frey, and Douglas Williams (2002, p. 72)

Imagine that you are a biologist on the first expedition to Mars. Your task is to look for signs of life, both past and present. Write a narrative about your search. Where would you begin your search? What signs of life would you look for?

Writing, in this instance, is a particularly powerful tool for helping adolescents listen, reflect, converse with themselves, and tackle both cultural messages and peer pressures.

—Peter Elbow (2004, p. 12)

Many newspaper and professional journal articles have been written about the excessive use of antibiotics to protect farm animals while they are being grown for market. Scientists know that the antibiotics will kill or inhibit most of the target microorganisms. However, some survive because they are resistant to the antibiotic. Write a narrative about the effects of this practice on bacteriological evolution.

Researchers helped us struggling teachers see that when students actually immersed themselves in the business of writing, they learned how to tackle ideas, play with language, and create structures that expressed their thoughts.

—Cathy Fleischer (2004, p. 25)

What does the phrase "survival of the fittest" have to do with biological evolution? What does *fittest* imply? Explain.

ANALYTICAL/EXPOSITORY

Inquiry treats writing as a problem-solving activity in which students come to understand something that they want to say before they begin drafting.

—Vicki Jacobs (2002, p. 60)

When Charles Darwin took his five-year voyage on the *H.M.S. Beagle,* he developed certain ideas about the evolutionary progression of organisms. Write an essay about the main ideas he developed during his voyage. Are those ideas still accepted today?

ANALYTICAL/EXPOSITORY

Reading, writing, and content learning are related.

—Douglas Fisher, Nancy Frey, and Douglas Williams (2002, p. 70)

NONFICTION WRITING FOR BIOLOGY

Explain the process known as *natural selection.*
How does this fit with Darwin's theory of evolution?

ANALYTICAL/EXPOSITORY

Citizens have influence only to the extent that they use it, and writing transforms an important but silent idea into a powerful source of influence.

—Douglas B. Reeves, Ph.D. (2002, p. 5)

Imagine yourself traveling 1 million years into the future. Write a narrative about how humans might evolve. Think about the evolution of plant and animal life. Will we still look the same? Act the same? What are some of the factors that could affect our evolutionary path (i.e., energy resources, water resources, etc.)?

The reason for the strong relationship between writing and test performance is unclear, but it probably relates to the relationship between writing and thinking.

—Douglas B. Reeves, Ph.D. (2002, p. 5)

What information about biological evolution can be drawn from fossils? What are some of the things we have discovered while studying the remains of ancient life? Explain your answer.

ANALYTICAL/EXPOSITORY

Bibliography

Boomer, R. "Speaking Out for Social Action." *Educational Leadership* 62, no. 2 (October 2004): 34–37.

D'Arcangelo, M. "The Challenge of Content-Area Reading: A Conversation with Donna Ogle." *Educational Leadership* 60, no. 3 (November 2002): 12–15.

Elbow, P. "Writing First!" *Educational Leadership* 62, no. 2 (October 2004): 8–13.

Fisher, D., N. Frey, and D. Williams. "Seven Literacy Strategies that Work." *Educational Leadership* 60, no. 3 (November 2002): 70–73.

Fleischer, C. "Professional Development for Teacher-Writers." *Educational Leadership* 62, no. 2 (October 2004): 24–28.

Jacobs, V. "Reading, Writing, and Understanding." *Educational Leadership* 60, no. 3 (November 2002): 58–61.

Perchemlides, N., and C. Coutant. "Growing Beyond Grades." *Educational Leadership* 62, no. 2 (October 2004): 53–56.

Reeves, D. B. *Accountability in Action* (2nd ed.). Englewood, CO: Advanced Learning Press, 2004.

Reeves, D. B. *Reason to Write (Elementary School edition).* New York: Kaplan Publishing, 2002.

Romano, T. "The Power of Voice." *Educational Leadership* 62, no. 2 (October 2004): 20–23.

Romano, T. *Writing with Passion: Life Stories, Multiple Genres.* Portsmouth, NH: Heinemann, 1995.

Saddler, B., and H. Andrade. "The Writing Rubric." *Educational Leadership* 62, no. 2 (October 2004): 48–52.

Schmidt, L. "Is There a Hemingway in the House?" *Educational Leadership* 62, no. 2 (October 2004): 42–45.

Vacca, R. "From Efficient Decoders to Strategic Readers." *Educational Leadership* 60, no. 3 (November 2002): 6–11.

Yancey, K. B. "Using Multiple Technologies to Teach Writing." *Educational Leadership* 60 no. 3 (October 2004): 38–40.

Yell, M. M. "Putting Gel Pen to Paper." *Educational Leadership* 60, no. 3 (November 2002): 63–66.